An Order of Service for Remembrance Sunday

*Commended by the presidents of the Churches Together
in Britain and Ireland:*
Most Revd Mario Conti, Catholic Archbishop of Glasgow
Revd David Kerr, Methodist Church in Ireland
Revd Nezlin Sterling, New Testament Assembly
Sr Eluned Williams, Methodist Church in Wales
Most Revd Rowan Williams, Archbishop of Canterbury*

CHURCHES TOGETHER
IN BRITAIN AND IRELAND

* Acting during a vacancy in the See of York, whose archbishop normally serves as president.

Churches Together in Britain and Ireland
Bastille Court
2 Paris Garden
London SE1 8ND

info@ctbi.org.uk
www.ctbi.org.uk

ISBN 0 85169 329 6

Published 2005 by CTBI

A catalogue record of this publication is available from the British Library

CTBI Publications
4 John Wesley Road
Werrington
Peterborough PE4 6ZP

Cover design and layout by Heather Macpherson
Cover photo by Phil Dickson

CONTENTS

INTRODUCTION:
An Order of Service for
Remembrance Sunday

This Order of Service has been prepared by a group representing the Churches and convened through Churches Together in Britain and Ireland, working in partnership with the Royal British Legion and the Joint Liturgical Group. It is commended on behalf of the Churches by the presidents of CTBI and replaces the service which has been in use since 1968.

The service is an act of Christian worship. In most communities, however, it will be appropriate for honoured guests representing other religious faiths and systems of belief to be invited. They will decide for themselves in which parts of the service they can with integrity join; planners will need to be careful not to make assumptions. The promise to work for peace, which forms an important element towards the end of the service, is deliberately not cast in religious language, to make it easier for people of other faiths and belief systems to be able to share in it.

The service as presented provides the entire order for a brief public Service of Remembrance. It will last about twenty minutes. It can, however, also be used as part of a longer service: either an ecumenical occasion or the regular Sunday service of a local congregation. When a sermon or homily is required, it would follow the New Testament reading(s). If the service is leading into a celebration of the Eucharist or Holy Communion, the transition would normally take place after the Act of Commitment from this service and into the other at the Peace or Offertory. Hymns and additional readings can be added at appropriate places.

Bear in mind the practicalities. If microphones are limited, consider how many people might speak without losing continuity and how the microphone is to pass from one to another. If wreaths and tokens are to be laid, think through the logistics of where and how, in order to maintain dignity without drawing out the ceremony for too long. When producing a printed order of service, it is helpful to include a reminder to people to turn off their mobile phones, and a suggestion that, as they gather, they wait in silence, so that those wishing to pray or reflect may do so. If the range of people to be present, and any organizations they represent, is known, it is also helpful for this to be noted.

If the service is scheduled to allow the two-minute silence to be observed at 11am, pay particular attention to the timing. The "Gathering" element of the service, if not rushed, is likely to take around four minutes. It is therefore wise to schedule the service to begin at 10.55. If that is not possible, it is better to omit most of the "Gathering" material than to miss the start of the silence at 11am.

THE SERVICE

GATHERING

All gather in silence

The presiding minister reads one or more of the following sentences:

Local custom will determine whether standards are to be brought and presented. If so, this should happen before any words are spoken.

God is our refuge and strength;

a very present help in trouble.

Psalm 46.1

I lift up my eyes to the hills –

from whence will my help come?

My help comes from the Lord,

Who made heaven and earth.

Psalm 121.1-2

If several sentences are used, they may be interspersed with silence or music. The amount of material used will need to take account of the time available. If used in full, the "Gathering" section takes roughly four minutes.

This I call to mind,

and therefore I have hope:

the steadfast love of the Lord never ceases,

his mercies never come to an end;

they are new every morning.

Lamentations 3.21-23

Those who wait for the Lord shall renew

their strength,

they shall mount up with wings like eagles,

they shall run and not be weary

they shall walk and not faint.

Isaiah 40.31

What does the Lord require of you

but to do justice, and to love kindness,

and to walk humbly with your God?

Micah 6.8

The presiding minister continues:

We meet in the presence of God.

We commit ourselves to work

in penitence and faith

for reconciliation between the nations,

that all people may, together,

live in freedom, justice and peace.

We pray for all

who in bereavement, disability and pain

continue to suffer the consequences of

fighting and terror.

We remember with thanksgiving and sorrow

those whose lives,

in world wars and conflicts past and present,

have been given and taken away.

REMEMBERING

When the service takes place other than at around 11am in the morning, local custom may suggest that the "Remembering" section should come later in the service, immediately prior to the laying of wreaths and other tokens. If so, before Binyon's words "They shall not grow old...", an introductory sentence will be required: "In peace let us remember"

An older person says:

They shall grow not old,

as we that are left grow old;

age shall not weary them,

nor the years condemn.

A younger person may reply:

It will often be appropriate for the younger person to be a relative – perhaps the grandchild – of the older reader. In some places local custom will require that both sets of words are said by the same reader.

At the going down of the sun

and in the morning,

we will remember them.

All affirm:

We will remember them.

The beginning of the two-minute silence may be signalled

The signal may be the chimes of a clock or bell, playing of the last post, or some other aural signal. In some places the radio broadcast of the chimes of Big Ben is used.

Silence

The completion of the silence may be signalled

The signal may be the chimes of a bell, playing of reveille and/or a lament, the reading of the Kohima Epitaph, or some other aural signal.

The following prayer is said:

Ever-living God

we remember those whom you have

gathered

from the storm of war into the peace of

your presence;

may that same peace

calm our fears,

bring justice to all peoples

and establish harmony among the nations,

through Jesus Christ our Lord.

Amen.

A note of penitence runs throughout the service. If, however, a specific act of penitence is required, it would fit most naturally immediately after the prayer "Ever-living God". The act of penitence from the 1968 service is included in the "additional resources" appended to this service.

*The following hymn, or another that
similarly expresses hope in God and
trust for the future, may be sung:*

O God, our help in ages past,

our hope for years to come,

our shelter from the stormy blast,

and our eternal home;

Beneath the shadow of thy throne

thy saints have dwelt secure;

sufficient is thine arm alone,

and our defence is sure.

Before the hills in order stood,

or earth received her frame,

from everlasting thou art God,

to endless years the same.

A thousand ages in thy sight

are like an evening gone;

short as the watch that ends the night

before the rising sun.

Time, like an ever-rolling stream,

bears all our years away;

they fly forgotten, as a dream

dies at the opening day.

O God, our help in ages past,

our hope for years to come,

be thou our guard while troubles last,

and our eternal home.

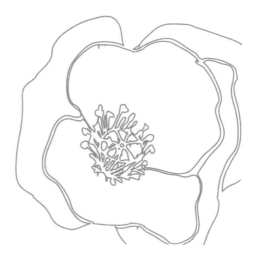

LISTENING FOR THE WORD FROM GOD

The reader says:

Hear these words from the New Testament

Or name the book, e.g. "Hear these words from the Gospel of John... and these words from the Letter of James"

Either *one or more of the following*

are read:

Peace I leave with you; my peace I give to
you. I do not give to you as the world
gives. Do not let your hearts be troubled,
and do not let them be afraid.

John 14:27

The wisdom from above is first pure, then
peaceable, gentle, willing to yield, full of
mercy and good fruits, without a trace of
partiality or hypocrisy. And a harvest of

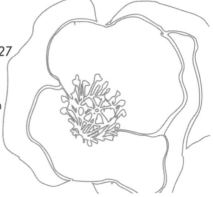

righteousness is sown in peace for those

who make peace.

James 3:17-18

This is the message we have heard from

him and proclaim to you, that God is light

and in him there is no darkness at all.

1 John 1:5

or *the following is read:*

When Jesus saw the crowds, he went up

the mountain, and after he sat down his

disciples came to him. Then he began to

speak, and taught them, saying:

"Blessed are the poor in spirit, for theirs is

the kingdom of heaven.

"Blessed are those who mourn, for they will

be comforted.

"Blessed are the meek, for they will inherit

the earth.

"Blessed are those who hunger and thirst

for righteousness, for they will be filled.

According to local circumstances, it may be appropriate to substitute one of the following for the reading set:

Psalm 23 **The Lord is my Shepherd**

John 14:1-8 **Do not let your hearts be troubled**

John 15:9-17 **Love one another, as I have loved you**

Romans 8:31-39 **Nothing will be able to separate us from the love of God.**

1Thessalonians 4:13-18 **You need not grieve like those who have no hope**

2 Thessalonians 2:13-16 **Stand firm**

Revelation 21:1-7 **Death will be no more**

"Blessed are the merciful, for they will
receive mercy.

"Blessed are the pure in heart, for they will
see God.

"Blessed are the peacemakers, for they will
be called children of God.

"Blessed are those who are persecuted for
righteousness' sake, for theirs is the
kingdom of heaven.

"Blessed are you when people revile you
and persecute you and utter all kinds of
evil against you falsely on my account.
Rejoice and be glad, for your reward is
great in heaven, for in the same way they
persecuted the prophets who were before
you."

Matthew 5:1-12

PRAYING TOGETHER

Prayer is led:

 Unless everyone has a copy of the service sheet, the one leading the prayers will need to inform the people of the response.

Let us pray for all who suffer as a result of conflict, and ask that God may give us peace:

for the service men and women who have died in the violence of war, each one remembered by and known to God;

May God give peace

God give peace

for those who love them in death as in life, offering the distress of our grief and the sadness of our loss;

May God give peace

God give peace

for all members of the armed forces who
are in danger this day, remembering
family, friends and all who pray for their
safe return;

May God give peace

God give peace

for civilian women, children and men
whose lives are disfigured by war or terror,
calling to mind in penitence the anger and
hatreds of humanity;

May God give peace

God give peace

for peace-makers and peace-keepers, who
seek to keep this world secure and free;

May God give peace

God give peace

for all who bear the burden and privilege

of leadership, political, military and
religious; asking for gifts of wisdom and
resolve in the search for reconciliation and
peace.

May God give peace

God give peace

O God of truth and justice,
we hold before you those whose memory
we cherish,
and those whose names we will never
know.
Help us to lift our eyes above the torment
of this broken world,
and grant us the grace to pray for those
who wish us harm.
As we honour the past, may we put our
faith in your future;
for you are the source of life and hope,
now and for ever.
Amen.

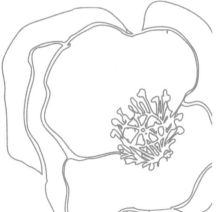

All join together in the Lord's Prayer: ◀ Or the version used in Scotland

Our Father, who art in heaven,

hallowed be thy name.

Thy Kingdom come;

thy will be done on earth

as it is in heaven.

Give us this day our daily bread

and forgive us our trespasses

as we forgive those who trespass

against us.

And lead us not into temptation

but deliver us from evil

For thine is the kingdom, the power,

and the glory

for ever and ever.

Amen

RESPONDING IN HOPE AND COMMITMENT

Representative and other members of the public come forward to lay wreaths, light candles or offer other symbols of remembrance and hope, such as single flowers or crosses.

How this is done will depend on local circumstances. There may be one area for official wreaths and another where any who wish are welcome to place symbols, either at this point or — if it proves more practical — as they leave the service.

The Kohima Epitaph is said:

Unless it has already been used to mark the ending of the two-minute silence.

When you go home

tell them of us and say,

for your tomorrow

we gave our today.

A hymn may be sung

The hymn should be an expression of commitment to service in the cause of justice and peace, of the kind expressed in the traditional hymn "I vow to thee my country".

19

The act of commitment is made:

The words of the Act of Commitment contain no religious references, and are intended to be usable by all present, whatever their faith or belief. They are followed by words in which those who are able to share in Christian prayer seek God's help for all who have made the commitment to live up to their promises.

Let us commit ourselves to responsible living and faithful service.

Will you strive for all that makes for peace?

We will

Will you seek to heal the wounds of war?

We will

Will you work for a just future for all humanity?

We will

Merciful God, we offer to you the fears in us that have not yet been cast out by love:

May we accept the hope you have placed in the hearts of all people,

And live lives of justice, courage and mercy;

through Jesus Christ our risen Redeemer.

Amen

The National Anthem(s) are sung

This will be the officially recognised National Anthem or Anthems for the nation in which the service is being held.

The following blessing is used:

God grant to the living grace,

to the departed rest,

to the Church, the Queen, the

Commonwealth

[or to the Church, the State]

The form in parenthesis is appropriate for use in the Republic of Ireland and other territories outside the dominion of the Crown.

and all people,

unity, peace and concord,

and to us and all God's servants,

life everlasting.

And the blessing of God Almighty,

Father, Son and Holy Spirit be with you all

and remain with you always.

Amen

ADDITIONAL RESOURCES

There are many additional new resources in the companion volume to this service, Beyond our Tears (published by Churches Together in Britain and Ireland on behalf of the Joint Liturgical Group, London 2004). A number of Churches also have material in recent liturgical publications, including the Church of England's *Times and Seasons* and the *Church of Scotland's Common Order*. There may be situations, however, where people wish to retain elements of the former 1968 service and similar services as an alternative to those printed in the present order. A selection is given below:

AN ACT OF PENITENCE

Let us confess to God the sins and shortcomings of the world;
    its pride, its selfishness, its greed;
    its evil divisions and hatreds.
Let us confess our share in what is wrong,
    and our failure to seek and establish that peace
    which God wills for his children.

After a short silence, all say:

**Most merciful God,
we confess that we have sinned**

in thought, word, and deed.

We have not loved you with our whole heart.

We have not loved our neighbours as ourselves.

In your mercy

   forgive what we have been,

   help us to amend what we are,

   and direct what we shall be;

   that we may do justly, love mercy,

   and walk humbly with you;

   through Jesus Christ our Lord. Amen

Almighty God have mercy upon us, pardon and deliver us from all

our sins, confirm and strengthen us in all goodness,

and keep us in life eternal; through Jesus Christ our Lord. Amen.

ALTERNATIVE INTERCESSIONS

In peace let us pray to the Lord.

We pray for the leaders of the nations,

that you will guide them in the ways of freedom, justice and truth.

Lord in your mercy,

Hear our prayer.

We pray for those who bear arms on behalf of the nation,

that they may have discipline and discernment, courage and compassion.

Lord in your mercy,
Hear our prayer.

We pray for our enemies, and those who wish us harm,
that you will turn the hearts of all to kindness and friendship.

Lord in your mercy,
Hear our prayer.

We pray for the wounded and the captive, the grieving and the homeless,
that in all their trials they may know your love and support.

Lord in your mercy,
Hear our prayer.

Most Holy God and Father,
hear our prayers for all who strive for peace,
and all who fight for justice.
Help us, who today remember the cost of war,
to work for a better tomorrow;
and, as we commend to you lives lost in terror and conflict,
bring us all, in the end, to the peace of your presence;
through Christ our Lord. Amen.

AN ACT OF COMMITMENT

Let us pledge ourselves anew to the service of God and our fellow
men and women: that we may help, encourage, and comfort others,
and support those working for the relief of the needy and for the
peace and welfare of the nations.

Lord God our Father, we pledge ourselves to serve you and all
humankind, in the cause of peace, for the relief of want and
suffering, and for the praise of your name. Guide us by your Spirit;
give us wisdom; give us courage; give us hope; and keep us faithful
now and always. Amen.

A PRAYER OF COMMEMORATION

Almighty and eternal God, from whose love in Christ we cannot be
parted, either by death or life: Hear our prayers and thanksgivings for
all whom we remember this day; fulfil in them the purpose of your
love; and bring us all, with them, to your eternal joy; through Jesus
Christ our Lord. Amen.

A PRAYER FOR THE ARMED FORCES

Almighty God, stretch forth your mighty arm to strengthen and protect the armed forces: grant that meeting danger with courage and all occasions with discipline and loyalty, they may truly serve the cause of justice and peace; to the honour of your holy name, through Jesus Christ our Lord. Amen.

A NOTE ON MUSIC

MUSIC RESOURCES FOR REMEMBRANCE-TIDE

Hymns

These hymns (listed alphabetically by first line) may be found in major hymnbooks such as *Common Praise, New English Hymnal, Hymns* and *Psalms, Rejoice and Sing, Church Hymnary Fourth Edition*, and the various collections published by Mayhew.

A mighty wind invades the world

Almighty Father, who for us thy Son didst give

Be still, my soul, the Lord is on your side

Christ is the world's true light

Eternal Father, strong to save

For the healing of the nations

God is our strength and refuge

God of freedom, God of justice

God with humanity made one

Great is thy faithfulness

Here from all nations

I, the Lord of Sea and Sky

In a world where people walk in darkness

In Christ there is no east or west

It is God who holds the nations

Jesus Christ is waiting

Jesus, Lord, we look to thee

Judge eternal, throned in splendour

Lead us, heavenly Father, lead us

Lord, for the years

Lord, save thy world; in bitter need

Now thank we all our God

O God of earth and altar

O God, our help in ages past

Peace, perfect peace

Pray for the Church, afflicted and oppressed

Praise, my soul, the King of heaven

Pray that Jerusalem may have peace and prosperity

Son of God, eternal Saviour

The kingdom of God is justice and joy

The right hand of God

Through the night of doubt and sorrow

Thy kingdom come, O God

To thee, O God, we fly

We pray for peace

We turn to you, O God of every nation

Will you come and follow me

From: Timothy Dudley Smith: A House of Praise

(OUP/Hope Publishing 2003)

Behold, a broken world, we pray

Eternal God, before whose face we stand (* specially written for

Remembrance-tide)

Remember, Lord, the world you made

From: Common Ground: A Song Book for all the Churches

(St Andrew Press, 1998)

What shall we pray for those who have died

We lay our broken world in sorrow at your feet

SONGS

Kum ba yah, my Lord

Lead us from death to life

Let there be love shared among us

Let there be peace on earth

Make me a channel of your peace

O Lord, the clouds are gathering

Shalom, my friends

TAIZE CHANTS

Da pacem, Domine

Christ of compassion (In te confido)

Dona nobis pacem

Dona nobis pacem, Domine

In God alone

Jesus, remember me, when you come into your kingdom

O Lord, hear my prayer

OTHER MUSIC

The RSCM has published a list of suitable choral anthems and organ music in Sunday by Sunday 25 (June 2003); see also Sunday by Sunday 33 (June, 2005). Details available from the RSCM website: www.rscm.com/sundaybysunday.

FURTHER RESOURCES

Copies of the Remembrance Service in this form may be ordered from CTBI publications as below.

Beyond Our Tears – resources for times of remembrance
ISBN 0 85169 286 9 £7.95 128pp (P)
Published by CTBI, available from bookshops and:

CTBI publications
4 John Wesley Road
Werrington
Peterborough PE4 6ZP

Telephone: 01733 325002
Fax: 01733 384180

Web ordering: www.ctbi.org.uk/publications

Postage and packing charges apply – please see the website for details.

Church of England Liturgical Commission: *Common Worship: Times and Seasons & Common Worship: Festivals*
ISBN 1 00 000 581 X £15 (published by Church House Publishing)
available from bookshops

Church of Scotland: *Book of Common Order*
ISBN 0 715206 84 2 £20 (published by St Andrew Press) available from
bookshops.